SQUAWBUCK JOE

SQUAWBUCK JOE

By
Duane Rossi

Edited by
Amy Nikolaus & Frank Diaz

This is a work of nonfiction. Any similarity between names and characters in this book and any real persons, living or dead, is entirely coincidental.

FIRST EDITION

Squawbuck Joe Copyright 2015 by Duane Rossi, All rights reserved. No part of this book may be reproduced or transmitted in any form or by any means without written permission from the author.

Published by Rossi Publications
Manufactured in the United States of America.

ISBN-13: 978-1523730100

ISBN-10: 1523730102

"Squawbuck Joe" book cover Graphic Design: Duane Rossi Copyright 1997. Most if not all photos within pages of this historical novel are from the private photo collection of Duane Rossi.

DEDICATION

This book is dedicated to Clifford K. Bowers, a proud American and grandson of Chief Joe Bowers. Clifford had the foresight to record this bit of local history, of which he was taught by his father, Grant Bowers, son of Chief Joe Bowers, and his mother Daisy. Squawbuck Joe was a friend to many Big Pine residents for years.

ACKNOWLEDGEMENTS

Acknowledgements for Squawbuck Joe go to the countless individuals who contributed their undocumented stories about the history of Owens Valley Paiute.

Anytime someone starts to write about Owens Valley history has to thank W.A. Chalfant for his well documented facts in the Story of Inyo. Thanks to my wife, Marie Rossi, for doing the typing, my daughters Mary Rossi, and Toni Jones, for the countless times they spent helping me with whatever with pictures and help with the computer and using the spurs to keep me going. Many thanks to Clifford Bowers, wife Mary, and daughters Tracey and Trudy Jo for letting me use the original story, Squawbuck Joe.

For all the rest of the pioneers and their stories of the early days that kept me interest alive my entire life. There is no way to thank them because most of them are over the hill now; but, I do believe I have thanked them on other pages of this book.

Sue Bobb and her Fry Bread: 4 cups Flour, 2 teaspoons Baking Powder, 2 teaspoons Salt. Warm Water. Mix dry ingredients. Slowly add warm water until you have loose soft dough, don't over work the dough. Put in a bowl and sprinkle with oil, then cover until ready to fry. Fry until golden brown in hot oil.

Sue Bobb's notes: Always smile, and never talk about water babies in the summer, especially while making Fry Bread -

To all those who read by camp fire light – the extra big lettering is for an EZ read.

Last but not least, I want to thank my good friend for many years as far back as when we packed mules in the Sierras. Without his help and expertise in the writing field I fear this book would have been delayed for quite some time. Thank you more than I can say, Frankie Diaz.

ABOUT THE AUTHOR

I was born in Bishop, California, and raised in Big Pine, just 15 minutes south. Much of my knowledge of the Paiute ways I got first hand from my neighbors. Our next door neighbors to the east were Rob and Emma Harry. I watched Emma make baskets and bead work, cook and shell pine nuts. Rob told us about the whippoorwills and rattle snakes. Next was the Bacoch family, Nick Jr., and Happy, were great athletes, I believe at another time and place they could have made it in major league ball. Then, there was Bob Piper and Maggie Piper; Bob made me a bow and three arrows when I was a boy, I watched him make it. Next were the Ross Stones. Vivian, Verna and Gina were the prettiest girls in the world.

On the west side of us, the family of Raymond Stone had resided. Raymond and my father worked for the Inyo County Road Department. When World War II broke out they built roads to the mines and kept them open summer and winter.

They spent much of their time on the Saline Valley Road, where they camped at Whippoorwill Flat. Meals were cooked in an old structure, called

Chris's cabin.

Over the hill to the east was the Wacoba pine nut camp. It was a large camp. There was a sweat house. One very large circle of rocks that had two or three inches of obsidian covering the ground. Raymond Stone told us it was how they stored their pine nuts the obsidian kept the chipmunks from digging them up.

There were several other rings all with an opening or door to the southeast leading one to believe they were shelters they lived in. The Calvary burned the camp so we don't know that the shelters were made of. In my opinion they were teepees like the one on the back cover. In my travels I have come across four of them.

The one on the back cover is in the lower end of Fish Lake Valley two of them on Westgard Pass and one by Marble Canyon. Raymond Stone later served in the US Army.

The Wacoba camp was covered by a flash flood. The Calvary had a mountain fort next to the Wacoba camp, and parts of the fort are still there. Our neighbors to the north were the Westervelts, Bakers, Wasson, Bowers, Tibbits, Sprats, a very artistic family, Stewarts, Sepsy, Pete Sepsy was the only one my age that spoke Paiute, and last but not least Claira Rambo and her Mother Aunt Minnie Piper who lived over a hundred years and was sharp in mind and memory until the end.

Fred Thompson was a Shoshone ancestry; he was born in Saline Valley, just east of the Inyo Range. Fred and I were partners working for Sierra Talc at the Ubahebe Mine at Hunter Mountain. We lived at "Gold Belt Spring"; Fred showed me how to catch doves and to always leave a foot on a rabbit. The cooking of desert animals was an art, which the Saline and Hunter Mountains tribes had honed for centuries. In one instance, Fred explained that if cooked correctly, Chuckwalla was better than fish.

I had to disagree, over a matter of taste, and how hungry a person had to be, in order to enjoy the retile.

Syless Ness who was born on the banks of Owens Lake told me of knowing a man who severely cut his foot while chopping wood. They doctored the wound with pulverized chuckwalla tail. The wound healed in a very short time. Sy also told me the correct name of Darwin Falls is Agee Pah (King Snake Water). My knowledge of crossing the Mojave Desert in a covered wagon was left to the family by my Aunt Stella.

In 1911, my Grandparents Tony and Nancy Rossi, traveled with their five kids in a covered wagon to see the ocean. Aunt Stella was eleven years old at the time and wrote a story. The melting pot corrals were built by Rafael and Tony Rossi, on the Rossi ranch six miles north of Big Pine on the old County Road. Most of the story is true and is well documented by W. A. Chalfant in the publication, *The Story of Inyo*.

PREFACE

While this story is fiction and some liberties have been taken in the chronology, most of the events are true and are well documented by W. A. Chalfant in the Story of Inyo. The Indian wars are true. The names of the pioneers and the places are correct.

There are a lot of wild stories about how Charlie Tyler was killed, but in 1954, Mike Rossi and the author were both home on leave from the service. We took a job with Arlie Brierley who was the County surveyor at the time. Arlie told us as young man he knew a very old Indian that was with the war party and when Charlie walked off the butte with his hands up a warrior shot him.

The story of Squawbuck Joe is true and has been passed down by the Paiutes from father to son and is very interesting part of early Inyo County history. The unknown period that he spent time in exile in the Inyo Mountains is not documented and may be fiction, but the pine nut camps and springs are all there and have been visited by the author. This is a good part of early California history and a very interesting read for any age.

Chapter One
THE LONG JOURNEY

Our story begins in the middle of the eighteenth century, in The Owens Valley. The Owens Valley is located in Central California on the east side of the Sierra Nevada. Captain Joe Walker, Jedediah Smith, Kit Carson and John Fremont had all explored the Owens Valley and found the Indians to be friendly.

The Valley was green and lush with many cold mountain streams running out of the Sierras into the many rivers and lakes; but, wildlife was very scarce. The one thing that brought the trappers and explorers back to the Owens Valley was the possibility of gold and silver in the Inyo range, east of the Owens Valley. Also, cattlemen were very interested in the possibility of starting ranches.

When the cattlemen and explorers returned to prospect for gold and silver they found the Indians living in the area not to be too friendly and they made it impossible to work the mines and be on constant guard against an ambush by the Indians at the same time. They had to leave their mines and call on the Calvary for help.

Governor Nye contacted General Wright and they sent fifty men to the Owens Valley. Captain Rowe of company "A" Fort Churchill, Nevada came into the Valley and brought fifty more men with him. Lieutenant Colonel George A. Evans came in the south end of the Valley from Los Angeles. They were joined by local cattlemen, farmers and miners.

Indian battles broke out from one end of the Valley to the other. Both sides were fighting for what they thought was right, but it didn't take long before the Indian fighting stopped. Some meaningless treaties were signed. Things soon calmed down in the Owens Valley and life went on. The Indians were not friendly, but they put up with the white men.

With the unrest in the East and the possibility of a Civil War brewing, the miners knew that silver and gold would soon be in demand. Land was free through the Homestead Act. This is when Joe Baker and his new wife, Katy, came to Inyo County and homesteaded land near Oak Creek.

They settled on a nice piece of land that was level and close to water. Joe had come from a large farming family in the San Fernando Valley and, being a young man with a new wife, he wanted his own farm and life. They brought two wagons and Katy, who was also raised a farm girl, could handle a span of mules with no problem.

One wagon was a covered wagon that they would live in it until they could build a cabin. This wagon was loaded with all the furniture and cooking equipment they would need for their new home. Katy brought a cedar chest and a small set of fine china her mother had given her for a wedding present. The other wagon was pulled by a large team of work mares that could be worked by voice and followed the lead wagon. Joe had thirty head of beef cows and one bull, two milk cows, four hens and one rooster, two house cats and one dog. He brought two hives of honey bees that he hoped to get established as there was no source of sugar in the Valley and honey would be in great demand. They also brought young apple trees in pots that would have to be kept watered, seed potatoes, onion sets and any vegetable seeds they could think of.

The trip was planned to start as soon as the feed started to grow in the spring because they could not haul feed for the animals, it also had to be early in the spring before the water holes dried up. Joe had made the trip the year before, carefully mapping the best feed, water holes and the routes they would have to follow. The route was fairly well laid out as Samuel Bishop had made the trip in 1861 with 500 head of cattle, 50 horses and established the San Francis Ranch on a large creek some 40 miles north of the site Joe had laid out. By all reports it was doing very well with very little trouble with the natives. The Magee family had been using the route with their cattle and Jess Summers had been coming down from the Bodie area and drove cattle to the mines in Mono County.

As the weather began to warm up the Bakers started to load the wagons, the stock they planned to take was parted out, the horses and mules were being fed corn, and the cattle were getting extra hay as they had to be in good condition for the long hard trip. They slaughtered a steer and hung the meat out to cool, the meat was wrapped in canvas and stored in the bottom of the wagons. The calves of both of the milk cows were big enough to travel so they would have plenty of fresh meat and milk to make the trip.

The morning they were to leave, the large family gathered at the breakfast table, Mr. Baker was at the head of the table and Mrs. Baker stood behind him and called for silence as she closed her eyes and prayed that Joe and Katy would have a safe trip and a good life. She gave Katy a bible and made her promise to keep a diary and to write home often. At last the time came for them to leave. Two of Joe's brothers would help them until they got to the high desert. The cats were put in a cage in the back where they could be fed and watered. The dog would help drive the cattle. With lots of hugs, tears and promises, Katy climbed up on the wagon, pulled by the mules. Joe got on the wagon pulled by the big mares and drove them up behind the first wagon.

Joe's brothers opened the gates and started the cattle, Katy slapped the reins and the mules started and Joe called for the mares to getup. Joe rode in front of the mules to lead the way, the cattle followed the wagons. Joe's brothers, one on each side of the cattle, and the dog keeping them moving in the back. They were on their way to a new home in a very wild new country with an unknown future. The weather was warm and the spring feed was coming on. There was a light rain falling, but this was always welcome and it would bring new green growth on the hills, it was called ranchers gold and was always welcome. As they started into the canyon, they noticed tracks of large wagons with very heavy loads. One of Joe's brothers had recently been to the Pueblo Los Angeles and the talk was that they were hauling bullion from a very rich mine in the Owens Valley by the name of Cerro Gordo. This was very good news to Joe as he planned to supply beef and vegetables to the mines in the area. They followed the tracks of the big wagons up the canyon.

Some of the cattle tried to turn back to the ranch, but the men knew how to handle cattle and the dog kept them moving. By late afternoon, they came to a small canyon that led off to the east with steep sides and good feed. They moved the stock up the canyon and made camp at the mouth of the canyon.

Katy had made a large stew at the ranch before they left. She got out her Dutch oven, made biscuits, and warmed up the stew. The cattle were tired and, after grazing awhile, started to lie down. After dinner, the crew was ready to bed down. They knew if any of the cattle came down the canyon, the dog would wake them up.

The rooster started crowing about four o'clock in the morning. The crew got up and built a fire and put on a pot of coffee. As daylight came, they saw the cows were up grazing and nursing their calves. The horses had gone up the canyon a little further, but came down when they called for them. After a quick breakfast of bacon and leftover biscuits, they harnessed the teams and saddled their horses and moved out for the second day of the trip.

They stopped at noon for lunch and to give the stock a rest. As they finished eating, a very big wagon, pulled by the biggest mules they had ever seen, came around the bend. The driver pulled up to the Baker camp and stopped. In the early days, all travelers stopped and traded information about travel conditions, feed, water, and trouble they may find ahead. Joe told the driver that his were the biggest mules he had ever seen. The driver, whose name was Dearborn, laughed and replied, "You see that wagon load of bullion? Every piece of bullion weighs 74 pounds and it takes a big team to pull it."

Bill Baker said he had been in Los Angeles a few days prior and was told they were hauling silver in from Cerro Gordo. " Is this some of it"?

"Yes, it is," replied Dearborn, "and you're going to see that little pueblo called Los Angeles grows into a big city. They are talking about building a pier in the port for a major seaport."

"Will you have some lunch with us?" Katy asked.

"No, thank you. The smelter is turning out bullion in Cerro Gordo faster then we can haul it. How is the road down the canyon?"

"No problem, you will make good time. How is it up the canyon?" Joe asked.

"The road is not bad. "Up near the top, you will see a large bluff of rocks, they are known as the Vasquez rocks," replied the man, "Tiburcio Vasquez holes up there and from time to time robs travelers. Are you well armed?"

"Katy has a double barrel shotgun beside her in the wagon and my brothers and I are well armed and are no strangers to trouble."

"You'll be okay. It was a wet winter on the desert and you will find good feed and water slicks until you come to the trail from the west that goes down to the Tejon ranch, then it will be dry until you get to Red Rock. I see you have water barrels on the wagons, so make sure they are full before leaving a water hole. Travel in the cool part of the day, morning and evening, try to find shade in the heat of the day. You have some fine looking beef there. You'll find a ready market for anything you can raise. There are mines opening up every place you look. Well, folks, I have got to get moving, good luck to you." The big wagon moved down the canyon.

"It sounds like that man has been around this country quite awhile."

"Yes, it does and his advice will be well taken."

"Although the trip was uneventful, pulling up out of the canyon was taking a toll on the stock. They took turns at night watching until they passed the Vasquez Rocks, but they saw nobody and moved on. A few more days and they were on the high desert and level ground at last. They found a flat that held water from a recent rain and laid over there for two days.

Chapter Two
THE HIGH DESERT

Joe's brothers would stay with them until they got to the trail down to the San Joaquin Valley and Fort Tejon. Mr. Dearborn had been right about the wet winter, there had been no trouble finding water and the desert feed was coming on good. From time to time, they had to help the teams pull the wagons through the wet places by using their ropes tied to the wagons and pulling with their saddle horses. But, they knew it would soon dry out as they journeyed north. They were making good time as the country was getting drier. There were a few sandy places where they had to use the saddle horses to help pull, but it wasn't much trouble.

The cattle were getting pretty well trail broke, so the dog moved them while the men helped with the wagons. They made camp before dark and that night two of the cows had their calves. They had planned on this and had room in the back of the large wagon to carry them until they were big enough to follow their mothers. After the calves were fed in the morning, they were put in the wagon and at noon they were taken out to feed again. At night they were left with their mothers until morning.

As they approached the trail that lead to Fort Tejon, they saw riders coming from the north. When the two men rode up, they introduced themselves as Elney and Bart Magee. They each led five mules and were going to Hart Flats for supplies. The Bakers wanted to know about the road ahead. The Magees, being some of the early pioneers in the Owens Valley were veterans of many Indian Wars as well as fights with bandits and every kind of outlaw you can think of - both two legged and four. The Magees looked the Baker's outfit over and said they would have no trouble.

Joe told them that his brothers would be going back the next day. Elney said, "In that case, travel slow. It won't take us long to get back. You'll be coming to Red Rock Canyon where the bluffs are red and white. You'll find water there, but not much feed. Do not go any farther, as you'll be coming to Robbers Roost, a large out cropping of rocks where outlaws have been staying and robbing travelers. We'll hurry as much as we can."

After breakfast the next morning, Joe's brothers did not want to leave, they said they would stay until the Magees returned. Joe said, "No, you have your own families and homes to take care of. You've done enough."

"Okay, we'll help you get the harnesses on and get started."

Once again, Joe said, "No, eat your breakfast, saddle your horses, get a cup of coffee, and sit on those rocks. Katy is fixing food for your trip home."

While Katy was putting the camp in the wagon, Joe brought in the horses and mules, got the harnesses on them and hitched them up to the wagons. He called to the dog to bring in the cattle. He saddled the horse he would ride that day and caught the two small calves and put them in the wagon. He drove the team of mares up behind the front wagon and tied the reins to the break handle. Joe and Katy walked over to the rock where the two men were finishing their coffee to thank them for all of their help. They told them to tell the home folks they were okay and that they where half way to their new home. Katy climbed on the front wagon. Joe got on his horse, called for the mares to get up, and called for the dog to start the cattle. One last goodbye and a wave to his brothers and they headed north.

Joe and Katy met another freight wagon that day heading for the Pueblo Los Angeles. They asked about the road ahead and Robbers Roost. The mule driver said that they had seen some activity at the Roost, but they were well armed and had no problems. He said the road was okay and the feed was good, but they would find no water until they got to Red rock canyon.

On the advice from the Magee brothers, they traveled slow that day. The north wind blew hard and the cattle didn't want to travel facing the wind and without water. They made camp early in the day. They had four fifty-gallon barrels of water on the sides of both wagons. They got a trough out of the wagon and watered the teams and the horse Joe would ride the next day. The cattle got the rest of the water, but it wasn't much. The cattle fed awhile and started bedding down for the night.

They didn't start until the sun was up the next day. As they came to Red Rock Canyon, they could not believe the beauty of the place with red and white bluffs carved for centuries by wind and rain. Katy made a note to describe the canyon to the folks back home when she wrote.

They would have liked to stay longer at Red Rock, but the cattle had smelled the water and headed out ahead of the wagons. When they got to the spring, they made camp. The first calves that were born were big enough to follow their mothers now, so Joe roped and tied them down. He heated up the branding iron and branded them with the JB brand. Two more calves were born that evening.

The weather was mild, the feed was good and they had plenty of water. All they had to do was relax and wait for the Magee brothers.

"I bet it sure gets hot here in the summer. You bet, that's Death Valley right off to the east. That's where the Jayhawkers thought they had a short cut to the goldfields. They lost all of their stock. A lot of the people lost their lives. They say it gets over a hundred degrees there, and there is no water

Chapter Three
RED ROCK CANYON AND
ROBBERS ROOST

A few days later, the Magee brothers rode into in late afternoon. They unloaded their mules. After dinner they sat around the campfire and told Joe and Katy of all the people they had talked to on their trip to Hart Flats, there was lots of talk about the Owens Valley. They explained that farms and ranches were being established throughout the valley, and a growing economy had farmers planting everything they could the Owens Valley was supporting itself with local trade brought by all sorts of enterprise.

The next morning they loaded up and started up the small grade out of Red Rock Canyon. The stock was well rested and it wasn't long before they were back on level ground. About an hour later they came in view of Robbers Roost. When they were about a mile from the Roost, Joe rode up beside the first wagon. He was to act like he was having some trouble. Bart Magee rode behind the covered wagon and got his telescope out of his saddle bag to take a look. "Yes, they're there alright. I can see seven or eight of them moving around."

They told Joe to stay on his horse to make sure the teams didn't bolt when they fired the rifles and Katy asked, "Are you going to kill them?"

Bart answered, "No, we're just going to fire a couple of shots to let those skunks know they better get back in their hole."

They fired the shots and Bart got his telescope and looked, again, "I don't see any movement, they must have got the message and took the warning. Let's head for Indian Wells, the folks there are a lot more friendly."

Indian Wells

When they rolled into Indian Wells there were people everywhere. There was a small Indian camp. There was a freight wagon from the north and there were teams that had come over Walker Pass. There was a string of mules with salted fish from the Kern River. There were a few women there, the first women Katy had seen since she left home. There were farmers, miners, loggers, merchants and trappers. There were pioneers heading for new country and they were all hungry for news. The Bakers couldn't stay long because there was very little feed, but they filled their water barrels. The Magees helped them get started and Joe thanked them for their help. Katy made them promise to stop by their new home and the Magees rode on ahead.. They were on their way to Little Lake.

Little Lake

It took the Bakers two days to get to Little Lake and what a site it was. It was no wonder this had been the favorite stopping place since the first white people, including the likes Jedediah Smith, Captain Walker, and Kit Carson had all camped at Little Lake. The natives must have camped there for centuries as there were petro glyphs on the rocks around the lake. There was a spring of good drinking water and plenty of water in the lake for the stock. The feed was knee high.

One saddle horse was staked out and the rest of the stock was turned loose to graze. Katy made a lunch and she and Joe walked over to the lake to eat their lunch. They both rolled over in the grass and fell asleep. It had been a long hard trip. They stayed at Little Lake for two days and pulled out the morning of the third day. The road was good, the stock was rested and they made good time. In the afternoon, they could see a small farm ahead.

Chapter Four
DUNMOVIN

As the Bakers came up to the farm, a man and woman came out to the road. There was a big sign reading "Dunmovin, Visitors welcome." Joe and Katy walked over to the gate to talk to the couple. They were very nice and eager for company and news. They were Al and Minnie Stewart. Joe looked around and said to Mr. Stewart, "It looks like you're pretty well set up here."

"Yes," said Al. "We have a little creek coming down out of that big canyon. Everything grows well in this desert if you get water to it. We have a few cows up the canyon and a big garden and chickens and a bunch of goats. The dogs have the goats out on the desert now. They'll bring them in before sundown. We sell meat, milk, eggs and vegetables. Katy told him she could sure use some fresh vegetables and eggs. "You folks are sure welcome to stay the night. There's not much feed, but we have plenty of water and we'll feed you dinner and breakfast for a dollar."

Katy said, "You got a deal." Joe started

unloading the teams.

Minnie and Katy were in the kitchen catching up on all the latest news and the men were sitting on the porch enjoying a glass of wine. They heard the dogs bringing the goats in, so they went out to put them in the corral.

"Have you seen any trappers heading this way?"

"Yes," said Joe, "there were some trappers camped at Indians Wells when we came through."

"Good, we can sure use them the wolves and coyotes are thick around here. If it wasn't for these big dogs, I wouldn't be able to keep any livestock here."

They had a big dinner of roast and lots of vegetables and talked well into the night.

By the time Joe had the teams ready to go in the morning, Mrs. Stewart had breakfast ready. They ate in a hurry and were ready to go. As they were shaking hands and saying goodbye, Joe looked around and said, "You folks sure have a nice place here, but it seems such an unlikely place to settle."

"Yes, it is, but there's just Minnie and me now, our two boys went back east to join Mr. Lincoln's army and our daughter married and moved on. We have family up north doing real good. They have sheep, cattle and a saw mill. We were heading that way to join them, but when we got here the wagon broke down and, Joe, I'm telling you we were dunmovin."

Chapter Five
OWENS LAKE

The road was good, but the grade was steep, as Joe and Katy left Dunmovin. Minnie watched through her telescope as they slowly made their way up the grade. When Al came in for lunch she told him, "Well, they made it to the top. Those are sure good teams they have. Soon they're going to stop for lunch."

After the noon stop, Katy noticed the cattle starting to go out ahead. She called to Joe and said there must be water ahead, the cattle are picking up the pace.

"Yes," he said, "there's a large lake. We'll be seeing it before long and it's called Owens Lake."

"Is there a town there?"

"Yes, two towns, Olancha and Cartago. Mr. Stewart advised me to get another dog, I'll see if I can buy one there."

Just before they got to Owens Lake Joe and Katy met two cowboys bringing cattle out of the foothills. They were the Carrascos who lived in Olancha and ran cattle in the summer in Monache

Meadows in the mountains to the west. They had two dogs herding the cattle and Joe asked if he could buy one. The Carrascos told him could have one of those, but, if he would stop by their ranch, they had a litter of pups that had been weaned and they'd be glad to sell him one.

Katy and Joe found the Carrasco Ranch and bought two pups, then continued their trek north. They came to a creek flowing out of a large canyon to the west. They made camp for the night under the large cottonwood trees growing along the bank of the creek. The next morning, while they were loading the wagons, they saw men using ox teams to pull Jeffrey Pine trees down to the lake. Joe asked what they were doing and was told that they had large kilns where they turned the trees into charcoal and sold it to mines to run their smelters. The drovers wanted to catch up on the news, but they were in a hurry to get a load of charcoal on the Bessie Brady to be shipped across the Owens Lake to the smelters at Swansea and Keeler. So, they said goodbye, wished them good luck, and cracked their whips and the oxen slowly started down to the lake.

They were making good time and Joe and Katy enjoyed the Owens Lake to their right and the most beautiful and highest mountains they had ever seen on their left. They passed by the north end of the lake and met a man with a loaded wagon. It was John Lubkin who had a ranch two miles up a small canyon to the west. He told them they would soon be coming to a lake by the name of Diaz Lake and, then, they would come to a town with a large pine tree growing by the creek. They call the town Lone Pine.

As Katy and Joe rode into the small town, they were amazed at the activity. Wagons pulled by both mules and oxen were traveling east, west, north, and south. Blacksmiths were busy shoeing horses and mules. Merchants were selling and trading on every corner. By the creek, a man had seven tied mules packed with large barrels. He had two young boys filling the barrels with water. Joe walked over and introduced himself. The man's name was Olivas. Joe asked him where he was taking the water and he replied, "I'm taking it to the mines."

"How much do you charge for water?"

"It depends. If I haul it to the top of the mountain, it's a lot. If I haul it to the base of the mountain, it's not so much."

Joe walked back to the wagons. "Did you hear that Katy? The water is free for the taking and he makes a living just hauling it to the mines. I'm starting to like this country more and more."

Katy looked at the peak there to the west. "They say its 14,996 feet high and call it Mount Whitney. What are those funny looking hills? They look like a pile of rocks."

"Those are the Alabama Hills. They were named by Southern Sympathizers that have gold mines up there."

Joe and Katy met two cowboys riding into town. Joe asked if they knew of a place that he could hold his stock for the night.

"Sure. We're the Elder brothers. Our ranch is just on the edge of town. We have a 40 acre field that you are welcome to use. It'll on be the right hand side, straight ahead."

Joe thanked them for their generosity, found the field without a problem, and turned their stock loose for the night. There were large shade trees where they could spend the night. As they were unharnessing the teams Katy said, "Joe, I noticed the sign as we came through town advertising the Spanish Garden Café. I could sure use a meal I didn't have to cook myself."

"Okay, Katy, let's clean up and ride into town and have dinner."

When the couple walked into the Spanish Garden, they were greeted by Mrs. Gamboa. She introduced the Bakers to her family, as they were all working there. Joe and Katy had a wonderful dinner and a pleasant evening. They rode back to the Elder field and retired for the night, ready for an early start in the morning.

A couple of hours after starting out, Joe and Katy came to an area with a few Paiute encampments and a large apple orchard and Joe said, "This is Manzanar."

"That's a strange name," Katy commented.

"Yes. It's Spanish for where the apples are."

They were pulling onto the land that would become their new home when Katy looked up at the Inyo Mountain range and asked, "What is that strange formation?"

"That's Winneduma. The natives have a lot of legends and stories about it. How do you like your new home?"

"I love it, but after that trip, anyplace would look like heaven."

Chapter Six
THE NEW HOME

As Joe and Katy were unloading the wagons, they looked up and saw a group of Indians watching them. Katy waved to them, but they turned and walked up the hill. "They don't seem very friendly."

"No," Joe said, "you can't blame them, but the fighting is over and things will get better. The first thing we better do is get the potatoes and onions planted and get the bees out."

The bees had been covered and were dormant on the trip. When they set the hives out in the sun and uncovered them, they could hear a buzzing sound. The sun was warm and the spring flowers were starting to bloom. Joe and Katy were smiling. They knew it wouldn't be long before they would have plenty of honey.

"Well, we better figure out where we want to build the house."

Katy asked, "Where are we going to get the lumber for a house?"

"Katy, look around you. Before we get this

property cleared we will have enough rock to build ten houses. We're going to have a rock house. Joe built a large sled that could be pulled with the mules and they started clearing the farm land. Each building-size rock was hauled to the building site. The flat rocks were set aside for flooring. The large rocks were used to make a corral for the horses.

Joe rode out every morning to check on the cattle and the loose horses and mules. Every day, he took one of the pups to work with the old dog and left the other one with Katy. He carried the branding iron with him so he could build a fire and brand the calves with the JB brand when they were big enough. The herd was getting bigger.

One afternoon, as Katy was working in her garden, she looked up to see a young Indian woman carrying a very large bunch of tules on her back. Katy waved, but the girl just looked at her and then hurried on to her camp. When Joe got home that day Katy asked him if he could take a little honey out of the hives. When Joe asked why, she told him about the Indian girl she had seen that day. "She was carrying a huge load and I would like to offer her some cool sweet tea the next time she comes by."

"That's nice Katy, but be very careful."

A few days later Katy saw the young girl walking down to the river, she prepared the tea and set it in the creek to cool. When Katy saw her coming up the trail she got the tea and walked out to the trail and sat on a rock. When the girl got near, she motioned her to come and have a cool drink. The girl came over very slowly and set the load of tules down. She accepted the drink and sat down. Neither women spoke. They drank the tea and stood up. Katy pointed to herself and said, "Katy."

The girl repeated, 'Kay – tee."

Katy nodded her head and pointed at the girl. The girl said, "Sui_Wah_Hee.

Katy could not pronounce the name and shrugged her shoulders. The girl picked a small flower, dipped her finger in it and made like a bird flying.

"Hummingbird." Katy understood perfectly.

When Joe came home that day, Katy told him, "I have a new friend. Her name is Hummingbird."

The Baker's farm was coming right along. They had a large garden and a pen for the chickens. Two of the hens were setting and two were laying eggs every day. The milk cow's calves were tied to trees and the cows came in every morning and evening to be milked. It was time to build the house.

Joe hooked up the wagon and went down to the river where he got a load of adobe mud. He brought it home and dug a pit to put the mud in. He added water and all the dry grass they could find and mixed it up to use for mortar. The building went fast, the fireplace was in one end and the front door in the other. A door was also left in one side for another room when they were ready for it.

Joe heard there was a sawmill operating north of them in a settlement they called Black Rock. They hauled the timber down from a mountain they called Shingle Bench. Joe hooked up the wagon and drove up there to buy a ridge pole, lumber for doors, and shingles for the roof.

When he was ready, Joe hired two Indians to help him lift the ridge pole. He gave them each a shirt and one half dozen eggs and they seemed well pleased when they went back to their camp. The roof went on fast and the flooring was next. They lit a fire in the fireplace that night and started moving the furniture in. They would have Mr. Dearborn bring them a cook stove on his next trip from Los Angeles.

That evening, Hummingbird came down with a basket of some kind of weed and gave it to Katy who looked puzzled and shrugged her shoulder. Hummingbird made the sign to drink and said, "Hebe." She motioned Katy to follow her. They walked out on the hill and Hummingbird pointed to a large green bush and made the drink sign again, saying, "Hebe." Katy learned her first Paiute word.

That night Katy boiled some of the tea and put some honey in it. Joe's eyes lit up when he tasted it. "I've heard about this Indian tea. It's wonderful. Why don't you give your new friend one of your dresses? I see some of the Indians starting to wear the white man's clothes."

Two of the saddle mares had colts and two of the hens had hatched out nineteen chicks. They sold all the new roosters and all but six of the young pullets. The cats keep the squirrels and rats under control. The young dogs would bark when a chicken hawk would come around the place and were trained to guard the garden and keep the rabbits out. The garden was starting to produce and every few days people were coming by, wanting to buy any produce Joe and Katy had for sale.

One morning, Katy saw Hummingbird heading down to the river. Katy waved to her to wait. She put a pack saddle on her mare and went to the river with Hummingbird. They gathered a huge load of tules and young willows. The tules would be used to make their shelters and bedding. The willows would be stripped of bark and used to make baskets. They took the load back to the camp. This was the first time Katy had been to the camp and she was a little nervous, but the natives seemed pleased with the help she gave them. She waved goodbye to them and returned to the farm.

Joe had to ride through the cattle everyday as there were herds being driven north every few days and he had to keep his own cattle separated from

them. There were miners hauling mills to be set up along the river to mill their ore.
There were prospectors with one or two donkeys heading up the hills. There was activity everywhere he looked. That night, when he came home, Joe told Katy about all the activity that was going on. "There's new settlement going in on that big bend in the river and they're starting to thrash wheat up by Bishop Creek. Our cattle are fat and looking good. Our farm is getting bigger."

Katy responded, "Joe, our family is going to get bigger, too. I'm going to have a baby."

Joe grabbed her and gave her a big hug. There was going to be a happy future for the Baker family in the Owens Valley. A few days later Hummingbird came down to see Katy. Katy ran out to meet her. She pointed to herself and then to her belly and made the sign of rocking a baby. Hummingbird laughed and pointed to herself and held up two fingers she was also pregnant. She made a sign for Katy to get her horse. They would gather willows to make two cradle boards.

One day, as Joe was checking on the cattle, he saw a wagon down by the river and rode down to visit. The party had been there for three days. Joe rode up to introduce himself, "I noticed you have been here for a few days what seems to be the problem?" The man's name was Wallace Partridge, he told Joe that someone had stole his mules. Two of their mules had been stolen and their wagon was too heavy for the remaining four to pull. Joe sold them two of his mules and helped them get on their way.

The Magee brothers stopped by the Baker farm on their way to Fort Tejon. They were very impressed with the new stone house. Katy cooked up a nice dinner for them and made biscuits in her new oven. They asked if they were prepared for winter. Joe showed them around the farm and how they were preparing for winter. The Magee brothers said it looked like they were doing very well . They told Joe to be sure he had enough supplies as the winters were long and hard and that there is a man named Tex Cushing who has dog teams that will come by with a few supplies when the snow is deep, but that's about the only travel you will see all winter.

Bart Magee were very happy to hear about

Katy's pregnancy and said, "You folks are exactly what this new country needs. But, you're missing a good bet by not raising mules. Everybody in the country is looking for mules. With those nice mares of yours, you could cross them with a jack and you will have all the mules you will need plus a ready market for all you can raise."

"That's a great idea," said Joe. Where can I get a good jack?

"When we travel south, we always camp on the desert with a sheep man by the name of Yribarren. We'll have him bring you a jack next spring when he heads north with his sheep."

"That sounds great, Men, thanks a million." The Magee brothers wished the Bakers well, and rode on.

Chapter Seven
DAYS OF THANKS

The days were getting shorter and it was starting to cool off in the evening. Joe lit a fire in the fireplace. Katy said, "Joe, Hummingbird tried to tell me something I didn't understand. She makes the sign for sun then she holds up both hands three times showing me she means thirty. She points to the mountains to the east and says Inyo, then, she looks like she is cracking a nut and eating it."

"She's trying to tell you she will be gone for thirty days. They're going to the mountains to gather pine nuts. I saw this when I came to the Valley the first time. The women will gather the nuts and the men hunt deer and mountain sheep. The young boys hunt the pine crows and chuckwallas."

"What in the world is chuckwalla?"

"It's a reptile like a very large lizard. They eat them like we eat fish. They don't eat the tail, they say when it's very dry they pound it into a powder and use it for cuts and wounds. They say its big medicine."

A few days later Katy saw the whole tribe heading for the mountains. Katy waved to Hummingbird and she waved back. Katy would miss her new friend.

The milk cows were giving plenty of milk. Katy and Joe made cheese and put it in the cellar to age. They had enough milk to make cottage cheese, butter, and buttermilk.

Ducks were starting to fly south for the winter. Joe took his shotgun down to the river and came back with four nice mallards. Katy cooked two of them that night. The feathers were saved to make into make feather quilts.

"Do you think we can have a goose for Thanksgiving?"

"There were lots of ducks today the geese will be here soon. I'll get a nice fat one. I heard a man by the name of Lewis brings four hundred pounds of fish into Lone Pine once a week. If I can find out when he brings them I'll ride down and buy some. The natives say there's fish in all the steams in the high mountains. I'm going to take our cattle to the high meadows in the spring. I hope I can find some fish. I sure wish I could bring some out alive and get them started in our creek. I heard they have done that up at the saw mill where we saw them hauling logs out. I think they call it Cottonwood Creek."

Joe and Katy had a small field of winter wheat and, hopefully, next year they could grow enough wheat to grind their own flour. In the meantime, however, they saddled two horses and rode to Bend City to buy some flour and a side of bacon. Katy made a sourdough starter and put it behind the stove to stay warm. They had ground some of their corn and made corn meal mush for breakfast. They ate it with fresh cream and honey, it was delicious and filling on cold mornings.

Thanksgiving morning, Katy roasted a goose. She cooked sweet potatoes and a winter squash with butter and honey and made a pan of sour dough rolls and a pumpkin pie. This was the first Thanksgiving in their new home. Joe said, "I wish the home folks could be here. I've sure been missing them today."

"Me, too," Katy said, "And I sure wish Hummingbird was here. But, no matter, if you can get me another goose I'll cook up a big dinner and take it up to her.".

Katy didn't have to wait long. The next day she saw the tribe coming up the hill. They had traded for two horses from a southern tribe. One horse was pulling a traverse loaded with pine nuts and the other one was packed high with meat. Katy was excited and sent Joe to the river for a goose. She spent two days cooking a huge meal. She had Joe put a pack saddle on her mare and they took the food to the camp and laid it out on a large flat rock. The chief walked over, he held up his hand and said a few words. Katy had no idea what he said, but she hoped it was a prayer for peace and thanksgiving. The whole tribe was smiling when Joe and Katy headed back to the farm. The next morning, when Katy came out of the cabin, a pottery dish full of pine nuts was on a rock by the door.

A few days later, Joe saddled his horse and two more horses and rode up to the camp. He told the chief with sign language that he wanted two young men to learn to ride and help him with his cattle. The chief called two teenage boys. Joe helped them on the horses and led them around the hills for a couple of hours and took them back to the camp. He pointed to the east and made the sign of the sun and pointed to his farm. The boys nodded, they understood. When Joe stepped out of the cabin the next morning, the boys were there waiting and eager to go. Joe showed them how much corn to feed the horses, how to brush them, how to put on the blankets and saddle, and how to bridle them. In a few days they could ride like the wind. Joe had all the help he would need to take his cattle to the mountains in the spring.

Christmas Eve came in with a foot of wet snow. When Joe opened the cabin door, he said, "Here is our gift from above, this wet snow on the winter wheat. We can grind enough flour to sell a few sacks.

The hens had stopped laying when the weather turned cold, but Katy had started heating up some corn meal with little chili peppers in it every morning to feed the hens and they started laying again.

When Joe came in that evening, wet and cold from feeding the animals and milking the cows,

Katy handed him a hot toddy made with fresh eggs, fresh cream, honey out of their hives and brandy purchased from Mr. Gerkin, who had a vineyard up by Bishop Creek.

Sitting by the fireplace after dinner that night, Joe said, "Katy, my gift to you this year is this farm and a new life in a new country."

"It's the best gift I have ever received and my gift to you will be a son next summer."

"Well, you topped my gift by a mile." said Joe.

Life was good on the Baker farm. On Christmas day Joe drove a steer up to the Indian camp. The Indians were gathered around a large fire. Some of them had rabbit skin blankets wrapped around them, but most had blankets that they got in trade with the white people. Joe pointed to the steer and made the sign to eat and yelled, "Merry Christmas." The chief yelled back. Joe didn't know what he said, but he knew the beef would be well used for a big Christmas feast. Katy had made Hummingbird new dress and the Indian girl gave Katy a small pair of moccasins for the baby.

Joe was starting to learn some of the words in

the Paiute language and his helpers were learning some English. But, for the life of him he could not pronounce their names, it sounded like they were saying "Little Bean" and "Jimmy," so that's who they became, Little Bean and Jimmy. They were becoming good cowboys. Some mornings Joe would stay home and let his helpers ride out to check the cattle. One morning Joe, Little Bean and Jimmy were checking on the cattle down by the river when a jack rabbit jumped out of the brush the boys yelled, "Camma." They grabbed their ropes and took off. Joe laughed until he cried, watching the boys trying to rope the rabbit, but he sure was proud to see how they had learned to ride and rope.

The trappers had been doing a good job controlling the wolves and coyotes. When Little Bean and Jimmy were out riding, and saw a wolf or a coyote on the flats, they would ride it down and shoot it with their bow and arrows. Joe showed them how to properly skin and tend the hides so, when the fur buyer came by, they could sell the furs for three dollars for wolves and one dollar for coyotes. Joe, also, gave them ten cents for every one they brought in.

The winter was long and cold, but Joe and Katy were well prepared and didn't mind a bit. In February a warm wind started to blow from the south and the snow was starting to melt in the lowlands. Joe said, "It's time to plant the winter onions. We'll plant the potatoes in March. Katy, I want you to ask Hummingbird if she can bring a couple of her friends down to help you with the garden this summer. Little Bean, Jimmy and I will be busy with the cattle this summer."

Spring was coming and it was starting to warm up. One morning Joe and Little Bean were checking on the cattle when a small bird flew up, Joe recognized the bird as a whippoorwill. Little Bean spoke with some English, some Paiute and sign language as he told Joe that the whippoorwill flies south in the winter. He told him the rattlesnake in Paiute is togo, and, like the bear, sleeps all winter. When the whippoorwill comes back in the spring, he wakes up the snakes.

A few days later, Joe saw a rattlesnake and Katy shot one that was in her garden. Joe thought Little Bean must have known what he was talking about and he would remember it.

The snow was melting in the high country and it was time to take the cattle in to the mountains. They put shoes on the horses and mules. They left early one morning. Little Bean and Jimmy showed Joe the trail over the Inyo Mountains to the Valley of Salt. It was a long hard pull when they reached the crest of the Inyos they stopped for lunch to rest the stock. Joe looked at the large pillar of rock that they called the Winnedumah. As he ate his sandwich he turned to Little Bean and said "Little Bean I heard a lot of story about this pillar of rock, what is the legend?" Little Bean had heard the story over and over, over the years. He started the story slowly telling Joe it happened many, many years ago when our grandfathers, grandfathers were still here. The Valley that the white people call Owens Valley was full of water. The people were giants in those days the Manaches lived on the Sierra side of the lake and the Paiute lived on the Inyo range. One day a huge Manache warrior saw two Paiute brothers climbing up the crest of the Inyo range he grabbed a lodge pole tree to use for an arrow with his mighty bow. When the bow released the tree sailed 15 miles across the valley and struck one of the Paiutes who fell faced down. The other Paiute started to run and the manache warrior hollered in a voice like thunder "Winnedumah" (which means stay where you are). The Paiute warrior turned to stone. Joe with a puzzling look, looked at Little Bean and Jimmie and said "Is this suppose to be a true story?" Little Bean replied "Of course it's true, see that lodge pole pine it's the arrow that took root and grew, it's the only one in the Inyo Range, how else could it of got here." Joe looked up at the huge pillar and stratched his head and said " Lets go down to the hot springs I will think about this later'

    Joe and the boys brought four mule loads of salt to take for the cattle in the mountains, some for their own use, and some to trade. They would take the work mares to the mountains so they could haul in logs to build a cabin where Little Bean and Jimmy could stay with the cattle all summer. They packed up plenty of food, axes, saws, and other building materials. Joe would load the horses and mules, Little Bean and Jimmy would herd the cattle. The old dog would stay to guard the farm and the young dogs would help with the cattle. They had just said goodbye to Katy and got the cattle lined out when they saw a flock of sheep heading north. Joe rode down to the camp. Sure enough, it was Mr. Yribarren and he had a young jack. The jack was broke to lead and had been packed. Joe tied him to his last pack mule and tried to pay the herder. The sheep man said he didn't need money, he needed vegetables. Joe told him to go up to the house. "You will see some women working in the garden. My wife's name is Katy and she'll let you in the cellar. Take whatever you need." They shook hands and Joe told him to be sure to stop when he came back in the fall. Joe had to hurry to catch up with the herd.

As they drove the herd up to the canyon, they noticed that a flock of sheep had gone in a few days earlier and they followed the sheep tracks. The cattle were in good shape and had no trouble. The second day, they rode into a huge meadow. They found a nice spot near a stream and wood to build a cabin. They unloaded the pack stock and Joe got a fire going and started to cook. The natives said, "No pugwee," and they went down to the stream. Joe watched as they got down and started running their hands under the bank. They were catching golden trout. Joe cooked the fish with potatoes and onions. They were delicious.

The next day they put the harness on one of the mares and pulled a large log out onto the meadow. With an ax, they made a salt log and filled it with salt for the cattle.

The log cabin went up fast with three men working on it. When it was ready, they put on the large tarp they had brought to serve as a roof until they could get one on. The cattle were doing great on the mountain feed and Joe was getting ready to return to the Valley. He told Little Bean and Jimmy to haul in a good ridgepole and to find a cedar tree and saw it into three foot lengths, he would bring in a shingle ax on the next trip so they could make shingles for the cabin.

Early the next morning, Joe took a pack mule up the hill and brought back a load of snow. He packed the golden trout in the snow and headed for home.

Chapter Eight
A SAD PART IN OUR LIVES

When he rode into the yard, Hummingbird and Katy were working in the garden. They were delighted with the fresh fish Joe had brought them. Hummingbird took half of the fish and got ready to leave. She had two rabbits that she had snared by the berry bushes. She had them skinned and cleaned. Joe noticed she had left a foot on both of them. When she left, Joe asked Katy why Hummingbird didn't cut those feet off those rabbits. "I asked her about that," she said. "The rabbit had to get to heaven."

"Seems kind of silly. A dead rabbit can't go anywhere on one foot."

"Joe, Christians go to church once a week and they worship one God. These people pray every day and they worship heaven and earth and everything in it, even the wind. It seems to work well for them and I don't think we should judge them."

After a dinner of trout and fresh garden vegetables, Katy said, "Joe, when you were gone,

Hummingbird and some of her friends went up in the hills and brought back baskets full of grubs. They cooked them in hot ashes by the fire and put them up for winter food. They called them pe agee. Then early one morning they went to the river and picked some kind of bugs off the willows. They used my oven to roast them they put salt on them and ate them like peanuts. They called them cauha."

"What did they taste like, Katy?"

"Well, I didn't eat one."

"What? After the scolding you gave me over the rabbit foot? I think it was very rude of you not to try a few of them."

"Joe Baker, you're impossible. If these golden trout were not so good I would throw one at you."

That night, as they sat on the porch watching the sun go down, Katy said, "Joe, my time is getting near, Hummingbird says not to worry, but I don't feel right .

"Okay, I'll ride down to the settlement on the river tomorrow. There are a few women there, I'll talk to them about it. I'd feel better about it too."

The next day Joe rode down to Bend City

When he walked into the General Store, the man behind the counter looked up and said, "Hi, there, Joe, how have you been?"

"I'm fine, but my wife's time is getting close and we're both getting kind of nervous about it. It's our first child and we're wondering if there is somebody around that might help us."

"Yes, there is, Joe. Stay right there. I'll be back in a minute or two." Fred came back with a small Chinese lady. "Joe, this is Mrs. Kong. Joe's wife is going to have a baby. It's their first one and they'd like to have some help."

Mrs. Kong nodded and says, "Come with me."

She led Joe down a hall in back of the store to a room with a bed on one side, a table with a washbowl and a pitcher of water and stack of towels and a big window on the sunny side. Joe looked around the room and asked, "Mrs. Kong, have you delivered a lot of children?"

"I bring lots of babies into the world. When Missy is ready, bring her here. I take care of everything."

They went back to the front of the store and Joe thanked Fred for the help. "No problem, Joe. And

Mrs. Kong is not only a good midwife, she is, also, a wonderful cook and a great seamstress and she keeps this place spotless."

Joe was in a hurry to get back to the ranch. He told Katy what he had found out and told her about Mrs. Kong. Katy said, "Thank you, Dear. I feel much better now. I'm not only excited about the new baby, I want to meet Mrs. Kong."

Joe was busy clearing more ground, he planned to double the size of his wheat field, he hauled the rocks up, he started building another room on the cabin, and it was time to take more supplies to the mountains. He was going to pack in a cook stove for the cabin. Also in the pack there was a double jack, shingle ax and nails.

Joe left before daylight the next morning. He rode into the high meadow that afternoon. The cattle were fat and lazy. Little Bean and Jimmy had hauled in a large cedar tree and had it cut into three-foot rounds. Joe was surprised about how many coyote furs the boys had on stretchers. When he asked them about it, they told him that one of them would hide in a tree while the other one would hide in the brush and squeal like a dying rabbit. When the coyote came to look, they shot it with a bow and arrow. Joe gave them the thumbs up. "You will have a good payday when we bring the cattle out this fall."

Flat rocks were hauled in so the stove would be level in the cabin. While the boys were cutting shingles, Joe boiled some Indian tea, cooked potatoes and wild onions with bacon and eggs. The roof went on fast and they cut a piece off the tarp to use for a door. They built two long benches, a long table, and a small table to set beside the stove. Nails were driven into the walls to hang the pots and pans. Next came the meat house. They built a platform up eight feet high so the bears couldn't reach it. On top they built a small room, leaving a two-inch gap between the logs. This would let the cool air in and keep the crows out. They built a ladder that they could take down when they left camp. They killed a steer that day and hung the meat in the new meat house.

Joe Baker loved the mountains, the cool air, and the green meadows. He cooked steaks every night and fresh trout every morning. He looked forward to the day he would bring Katy and the new baby in to see and enjoy it. With Katy's time getting near, he started getting ready to leave. They caught more fish for him to take out. He packed up and headed back to the Valley.

With the help of natives from the camp, Joe was able to finish the new room on the cabin. They moved the baby's cradle in and Katy got out the cradle board that Hummingbird had made. They put a rug on the floor of the new room and curtains on the windows. They were ready for the new baby.

The days were very warm and Katy and Hummingbird spent most of the day sitting in the shade by the creek. Katy was teaching Hummingbird how to make her own dresses. They were, also, sewing some small blankets for the babies.

When Joe Baker wasn't busy with the farm, he was hauling fresh vegetables, milk, eggs and cheese to sell at the settlement on the river, to the mines, and to the mills being built in the foothills. The weather was hot, but comfortable and business was good.

One day Katy said, "I haven't seen

Hummingbird for three days, I wonder if she has had her baby?"

"I wouldn't doubt it. Your time is near, too."

By late afternoon, Katy was not feeling well and went to lie down. Joe asked if she would like to go to the settlement. "No, if you will make me some tea, I'll rest awhile."

"Well, I'm going to harness the horse and have the wagon ready."

Katy still wasn't feeling well that night and did not eat dinner. Joe said, "I'm taking you to the settlement the first thing in the morning."

Katy nodded her head and fell asleep. Joe was worried as he blew out the light and went to bed with his clothes on. During the night he was startled by Katy, "Joe, something is wrong, I'm very sick."

"I'll get you to the wagon."

"No, Joe there's no time. The baby's coming."

She was right. Joe had always helped the young mares when they foaled and the heifers with their first calves, but his own child was something that never entered his mind. Katy was so weak he could hardly hear her mumbling. He bent close to her ear and said, "Katy, we have a son."

Katy opened her eyes and tried to smile. She whispered, "Joe I'm not going to make it. Please, name the boy after my father, Walter." She dozed off. By morning, Katy was gone. Joe was in a daze. During all the planning and building they had done, this was something they had never talked about. The baby was crying and hungry. Joe heated some milk and dipped in a clean dish rag and had the baby would suck the milk out. Joe knew this was not enough and he needed help. He put the baby in the cradle board, saddled his horse, and carried his newborn son to the Indian camp. Hummingbird heard the baby crying long before Joe got there and was waiting when Joe rode into camp. He told her what had happened in English, but Hummingbird understood him and she took the baby to her breast, where he would stay for two years.

The Chief sent two men with Hummingbird and two of her friends to help Joe with burial arrangements. The women wrapped Katy's body in a beautiful rabbit fur blanket and told the two men to dig a grave under the oak trees by the creek where Katy and Hummingbird had spent so many pleasant hours.

Joe spent a long sleepless night worrying what to do. The demands of the farm would not let him grieve too long. He buried himself in work. His duties were double now and he was sure he could get all the help he needed to work the farm He took a milk cow up to the camp and tied her calf to a tree, he explained that the cow would come back every morning and every night to feed her calf and to be milked. Hummingbird had helped Katy milk and knew all about it.

The next morning, people started showing up at the ranch. There were miners, farmers, cowboys, and hunters. People from miles around came in wagons, on horseback, and on foot. Joe was amazed and asked Charlie Tant, an old lion hunter, how so many folks got the news so soon. "It's the moccasin hot line, Joe. The natives have used it for centuries. They send their fastest runners in all directions and the next tribe does the same. This here is a local deal, but if they had wanted to, you can bet the word would have been spread from Mexico to Canada in a very short time."

Some of the men went to the barn and made a coffin and the women lined it with one of Katy's blankets. They placed Katy's body in the coffin and nailed on the lid. Nine native women, lead by Hummingbird, circled the casket. She hung Baby Walter in his cradle board on a limb nearby and returned to the circle. She held up her hands and pointed in all four directions and then to the heavens. The whole tribe was standing by and they started crying all at once. Some of the women cut off their hair and laid it on the coffin. This went on for a few minutes. Hummingbird carried Baby Walter back to the circle. The women passed the child back and forth across his mother's coffin three times. The crying stopped and the women quietly went back to stand with the tribe.

Bart Magee walked up next. "I met Joe and Katy a few years back, when they first came to this country. I knew they had big plans, but to look around and see what this young couple did working together is unbelievable. And the most amazing thing is how they have come together with the natives. With this terrible war going on, in the east brother against brother, the world could use more people like the Bakers. Ten years ago if somebody told me that a whole tribe would be crying over a white person, I would not have believed him."

Jess Summers was next to talk. He said he had dealt with the Bakers since they first came to the Valley and like Bart he was amazed at what they had accomplished. "There is not a lot of pleasure in this wild country, but when you rode up to the Baker ranch, Katy's smile would light up the day. She always had a pot of coffee or tea on and a pot of stew. Nobody ever left the ranch hungry. Well, folks you know that I'm not a preacher not even close to being a preacher and my religion has kinda left me through the years, but I believe someday, somewhere I will meet Katy again and see that beautiful smile. Like I said folks, my religion has kinda left me, but I want to now say when the sun sets on the Sierra, the last day I'm on earth, I don't want a lot of crying' and flowers. I've been happy since the day of my birth. I've had a lot of good friends go on down the line, and I know when I get there we'll have a mighty good time. Now, don't get me wrong, Lord, I like it here just fine, but sometimes I get to missing' them ol' pals of mine. We'll sit around on a sunbeam, and lean back on a cloud. We'll have a drink of heaven's brew, me and that old crowd. We'll talk about the things we've done, and the times that we were here. We'll catch a lot of fish, and we'll shoot a lot of deer. We'll talk about the mules we packed and the ones that were tough to shoe. And, Pard, we'll even talk a time about you. We'll talk about our trap lines, the ones we ran in the snow, and how they ripped us off at the sale, But, that's forgiven now. We'll talk about our families and how tough it was to go, But, they'd feel a lot better if they could see us now. From cradle to grave is such a very short span and we're all gonna go there, animal, plant, and man. So when that sun sets on the Sierra and that river runs around the bend. I don't want any cryin and flowers. I'll be with a bunch of my friends."

A silence fell over the group, but the ladies started bringing out food and setting it on the tailgates of the wagons and on the large flat rocks by the cabin door. Hummingbird had a fire going in Katy's cook stove and brought out several large pots of coffee. After the meal, the women started putting everything back in the wagons, preparing to leave for their homes. The men gathered around Joe Baker offering their condolences and making him promise that if he needed any help with the ranch or cattle, to let them know. After everyone left, Joe sat quietly in the yard. He was overwhelmed by the generosity of his friends and neighbors. He knew he couldn't grieve very long because it was almost time to bring the cattle out of the mountains.

Joe went to the camp to ask Hummingbird to take care of the garden and to use whatever they needed. He said goodbye to Baby Walter and got ready to go to the mountains.

Little Bean and Jimmy were doing fine and the cattle looked good. Joe told them what had happened and told them to start bringing the cattle down to the big meadow because it was almost time to bring them down to the Valley.

Chapter Nine
HARVEST TIME AND COW CAMP TIME

The hunters and trappers had been very busy, they had almost eliminated the wolves and were getting the coyotes, lions and bears under control. They were starting to see a few coveys of quail in the foothills and Joe had seen some deer tracks along the creek. Hummingbird was having a hard time trying to get her chores done while carrying two babies, but Joe gave her Katy's mare and she would tie one cradle board on each side. She could now go to the river to do her gathering and work in the garden with no problems.

The wheat was ready to harvest. When Joe came down from the cow camp, Hummingbird brought her friends down. Joe cut the wheat with a sickle and the women gathered it up and laid it out in the sun to dry. When it was dry. they shook the stems and the wheat would fall into their large baskets, then they would throw the grain high in the air, the wind would blow the small stems away and the clean wheat would fall back into the basket. Joe got out the hand grinder and they ground the wheat into flour.

Joe got out the sourdough starter. He mixed the starter with some flour and a little water and gave half to the women. He went in to start a fire in the cook stove to make some bread. A few days later, when the women came to work, they brought Joe some bread they had made, It was flat and cooked golden brown and looked delicious.

The Magee brothers came by and Joe was fixing them lunch. He put beans on the Indian bread. He cut up onions, tomatoes and chilies and put them on top of the beans. Bart asked Joe, "What kind of bread is this?'

"I call it Indian fry bread. Try it, I think you will like it." And they sure did.

"Joe, we will make sure it's time to eat every time we come by from now on."

"I sure hope you do. It gets awful lonesome here without Katy."

Jess Summers came by and wanted to buy Joe's cattle when he brought them out of the mountains. Joe said, "They'll be ready before long and I want to trade you for a new bull." Jess told him he had bulls up at Warm Springs and he would bring one down on the next trip.

The Indians were getting ready to head up to the mountains. Hummingbird had made arrangements for some elders that would not be going on the trip to take care of the farm when Joe went in to bring the cattle out. The next morning, the Indians came down the hill and Joe walked out to say goodbye to little Walter. He was kind of worried, but he knew the baby was in good hands.

The next morning, Joe rode up to the camp and told the elders to feed the chickens and gather the eggs. He tried to pay them, but they told him that all they wanted was the eggs. Joe left the old dog to watch the place and to keep the varmints out of the garden. He called the pups and headed for the cow camp.

When Joe rode into camp, he was surprised to see a deer hanging on the meat pole. When he got his stock taken care of, he skinned the deer and cut some steaks for dinner. He laid the hide out to dry.

It wasn't long before Little Bean and Jimmy rode in with a few head of cows they had located on one of the higher meadows. They ate dinner and

Joe asked about the deer. Little Bean said, "Tyee." He licked his lips and rubbed his belly. The boys said there were a few deer showing up.

In the morning, Joe and the boys put up jerky lines. They cut the meat into strips, salted it down, and hung it up to dry. Now, they had time to do some hunting. Joe shot a nice buck with his rifle and two days later Jimmy got one with his bow. As soon as the meat was dry, it was taken down and more was hung up. They were, also, drying fish. They were enjoying the hunting and fishing, but the nights were getting cold. The aspen trees were turning red and gold and there was ice on the water bucket in the morning.

Joe and the boys counted the cattle everyday and were sure they had them all. It was time to start getting ready to leave. Everything they were going to leave was stored in the meat house for the winter. The packs were made up ready to load on the mules in the morning. It snowed that night and while Joe was cooking breakfast. Little Bean and Jimmy rode through the cattle to make sure all the cows were up and the calves had been fed. They were soon packed up and ready to go.

They tied the door open and poured pepper around and on top of the stove to keep the bears away. They were ready to go.

The cattle were started and headed down the canyon. Every cow had her calf. At noon they held up the drive to let the cows find their calves and feed them because it's a natural instinct for a lost calf to go back to the last place it had fed and the cow will return to the place where she last fed her calf. They would do this several times on a drive. They called it "mothering up" and it saved a lot of time going back to find a lost calf.

The herd was held up again when they reached the valley floor and the cattle were left on the river. The old dog came out to greet them as Joe, Little Bean, and Jimmy rode into the farm. Smoke could be seen up at the camp and they knew the tribe was back from the mountains. Joe put some of the jerky and fish in the cellar and told Little Bean and Jimmy to take the rest to the camp. He would be up to see Walter when he got unloaded and the house opened up.

Joe could not believe how much Walter had grown in such a short time. The camp was busy and happy, the children were running and playing, the women were weaving baskets, and the men were making bows, arrows and arrow heads. Others were tanning deer hides to make moccasins. Some were tanning rabbit skins to be made into robes and blankets. The chief came over and thanked Joe for the jerky and fish. They had a very good year at the Wacoba camp and had brought loads of nuts and jerky back with them. The Indians had, also, stashed a large amount of pine nuts in a circle of rocks and covered them with a layer of obsidian so the squirrels could not dig them up. Little Bean and Jimmy were relaxing beside the fire when Joe told them he would need them the next day.

Joe and his helpers roped the two biggest colts and led them back to the farm. The colts would be gentled down and used as pack horses when they went to the mountains in the spring.

Jess Summers came to the ranch a few days later with the new bull. They rounded up the cattle and Joe parted out the heifers that he would keep. The steers were sold to Jess. One old cow that didn't look like she would make the winter, so was drovin back to the farm to be made into corn beef.

Joe Baker stayed busy on the farm. He dug the potatoes and onions and picked the melons. He stored what he would use in the cellar. The rest of his produce was put on straw in the wagon. He harnessed the team and headed for a large mill they were building on the river. The river was low this time of year and he had no trouble crossing. When he pulled up to the mill, he sold everything he had brought in his wagon. The two things most in demand were flour and honey. Joe had six hives producing now and planned to get a new swarm out of each hive in the spring. He planned to double the size of his winter wheat field. Joe knew of a man by the name of Jones, up in Round Valley, who has a water-driven grinder. He would haul his wheat up there next year to be ground into flour.

The sheep men were bringing their sheep down from the high country, heading for the desert for the winter. The herders were of all nationalities and were lonesome and ready for company. The French had the best wine. The Basque made the best lamb stew. The Italians all played their accordions and would play and sing every night. The Mexicans liked hot chilies and gave Joe some seed. Joe promised to have peppers for them when they come next year. The Rossi's had established a homestead on the west side of the valley between Big Pine Creek and Bishop Creek. They had a nice vineyard started. Tony was taking his sheep to the desert for the winter and brought Joe some grape shoots to be started on his farm. Tony said, "Joe, these are cuttings from Muscat grapes. We brought the cuttings from Monterey, over on the coast, when we first came to the valley. They're a large grape and fast growing. We always add a couple of handfuls of the Muscats to our Burgundy. It makes a very fine wine. Try it, I think you'll like it. We call it Rossi's Mellow Burgundy." Joe accepted the gift on the condition that Tony would stop and have a glass of wine with him every time he came by. All the herders could speak Spanish and, being a native Californian, Joe could speak it, too. But, he always wanted to learn a few words in the native language and he would teach them a few words in English and a few words he had learned in Paiute.

The one thing they all had in common was they loved this new country.

There were no holding corrals in the valley, so Joe spent the next month building large holding pens and camp sites in a grove of trees on the lower part of his farm. The site was free for all to use and it wasn't long before it became the meeting place for travelers from all over the world who had come to America for a new life. They made big fires at night and shared their meals and travel news. Some got out there banjos and fiddles and they sang and danced far into the night. Tony Rossi played his accordion and entertained the group with the Irish Washer Woman, an Irish jig he had learned in New York when he first came to America. He played the National Anthem and Over the Waves. He ended the evening by playing The Girl I Left Behind and that brought tears to the eyes of many of the lonesome travelers. Joe enjoyed the company and called the camp a melting pot.

Winter came hard that year and the wind blew for days. Snow was deep and the cattle were doing their best to find enough feed to stay alive.

Joe would bring Walter to the cabin and rock him in Katy's rocking chair, but Hummingbird insisted he take the baby back before dark. Joe had time to write home, but getting mail out was a problem. Tex Cushion would come by with his dog teams and stay a few days. The nights were bitter cold and the winds howled during the day. Joe Baker said " Why don't you stay a few days Tex. I have plenty of room and feed for the dogs. The mail can wait." Tex said "Thanks Joe, I know the mail can wait but I have some medicine for Mrs. Cashbaugh." Joe said "I haven't met the Cashbaugh's yet." Tex said "They are German immigrants, hard working, some of the first people in the valley. They have a ranch on lower Bishop Creek and also holding in Long Valley where they summer their cattle. They part off their beef cattle in the fall and drive them to markets of Mono County saves over a hundred miles on the fall drive. Then they bring their cows back to Bishop Creek for the winter. I don't know how much they need this medicine so I am going to bundle up and head north." The travelers that did come by, pulled large sleds with their teams hitched in line.

Christmas had come and gone and the long cold winter hung on. Joe was missing Katy. He sat by the fire day after day. He was thinking he would take Walter in the spring and leave the valley. When Little Bean and Jimmy came in the cabin the next morning they asked Joe if he was sick, "No, boys, I think I'm just lonesome. I'm thinking about giving you boys the ranch and leave the valley."

The boys got up and went back to the camp. They returned shortly with the chief and Hummingbird with her son and Walter. When they walked, in Joe was still sitting by the fire. "Joe Baker, you cannot leave." The chief spoke in Paiute, but Little Bean and Jimmy knew enough English to translate. "Look at your fine son and you could never find a better women to help you raise him. Look at these two boys you have helped become good hard working cowboys. You have helped the miners, the travelers, and the settlers. The help you have given the tribe has made our lives a lot better." The chief walked to the door and said, "Kema."

They all walked out to the yard. The morning sun was up in the East and the full moon was up in the West. The chief pointed to the sun and moon and said, "Phavee, everything is good."

Joe looked over at Katy's grave. The snow was starting to melt. A smile came on his face and he knew he would not be leaving anytime soon.

Joe was looking forward to spring. Walter and his adopted brother had outgrown there cradle baskets and were starting to crawl. Joe would bring them to the cabin and Hummingbird would let them stay overnight from time to time.

The civil war had come to an end. Veterans, both north and south, were coming to the Valley. The Union vets were put out when they learned the South had named the hills west of Lone Pine the "Alabamas" for the privateer who sank the Kersarge. When the Union vets located a very rich mine high up in Sierra, west of Camp Independence and looking down on the Alabama Hills, they named the mine "The Kersarge." There were some hard feelings on both sides, but Joe noticed when the music started at the melting pot corrals a lot of hard feelings were forgotten.

Little Walter and his adopted brother were growing like weeds and starting to talk. Not all native children were given names at birth and many of them earned their names later such as Night Stalker, Butcher Knife or Fastman. Walter didn't know what to call his adopted brother, so he started calling him "Little Joe" like his father and the name held for the rest of his life.

The elders were teaching the boys how to make traps with flat rocks and how to set snares for rabbits. Joe Baker was teaching them how to take care of the garden and to tend to the animals on the farm. The little boys were busy on the farm and at the camp.

Chapter Ten
A WAY OF LIFE EARLY SPRING

The weather was warming up and Little Bean and Jimmy went to the Valley of Salt and brought back several loads of salt. Then, they rode north and packed back loads of obsidian. The obsidian was used to make scrapers for tanning hides, and to make knifes for skinning, tomahawks, spears, and arrowheads. Obsidian was in great demand for the southern tribes and they traded colorful beads for it. They used it for barter, to decorate their ceremonial items, and to make necklaces. They wove it into their clothing

Large pieces of obsidian were broken into smaller sizes. The nappers would hold the small piece with buckskin and, with a deer antler, make it into an arrowhead. a knife, or, sometimes, an ornament to be worn around the neck. Not all the natives had the skill, but those that did often were given the names such as flint man or arrow maker. These men were the most important members of the tribe. Before the natives could trade with the white men they were responsible for supplying all the tools and weapons for the tribe. They, also, made ornaments to be offered to the spirits in prayer.

The men who made the bows and arrows also were very important to the tribe. The bows were made from willows that were soaked in water, then dried in the desired curve and strung with buckskins. Arrows for small animals were made from the cattail. Willow was used to make arrows for the larger game. They used hardwood that was soaked in water and dried perfectly straight. They rubbed the arrow shaft smooth with a stone called an arrow straightener. Feathers of the eagle and duck were used for fletching. The hardwood arrows were fitted with arrowheads and the light arrows were fitted with a variety of points, depending on the game they were hunting.

It was soon time to take the cattle in the high country for the summer. Joe Baker let Little Bean and Jimmy shoe the horses and mules. They had a little trouble getting the salt packed on the young colts, but they soon settled down. He even let them pack the food. They wouldn't need much. With all of the deer and grouse they had seen last summer, plus wild onions and trout, all they needed was potatoes. They packed heavy cable for snares. They picked a large amount of tea.

Joe Baker lead the pack stock and Little Bean and Jimmy started the cattle up the canyon. The spring feed was coming good when they got to the meadow. There were bear tracks everywhere, but the pepper had kept them away from the stove and nothing was disturbed. In the morning, they had a late breakfast of fish. They moved the cattle around to the smaller meadows and filled the salt logs. They saved the feed in the big meadow for the fall, when they would gather.

Jimmy had set a snare in a trail above the cabin. When they rode into camp that afternoon they could hear a big commotion and a lot of growling. They knew they would be eating fresh bear steaks for dinner. The choice cuts of the bear were hung in the meat house, the rest was made into jerky. The hide was laid out to dry.

Joe Baker could not stay as long as he wanted to and soon went back to the farm. When he rode up to camp to see Walter and to deliver the fish he had brought, he also had two bear hides. Some of the natives were getting rifles and learning how to use them. but most were still using bow and arrows and the bear hides were highly prized.

The farm was doing very well and Joe Baker was hiding his gold around the farm. There was always word of bandits around the valley. He wanted to get the gold into a bank and was planning a trip south to deposit the gold. He, also, wanted to introduce Walter to his grandparents. He had his work cut out for him.

When the boys came running into the house that evening, as wild and hungry as young wolves, they were stopped in their tracks. Joe Baker had gotten into Katy's hope chest and had the table set with linen and fine china. He said, "Boys, go to the creek, wash your hands and face and comb your hair." At the end of a week the boys knew how to use a knife and fork and when to say please and thank you. Joe trimmed their hair and got out their best cloths.

Joe Baker had bought a light buggy and the young horses were broke to harness, so they would make good time. They packed what food and bedding they would need and were on their way.

When they pulled out of the yard, Hummingbird was standing in the road. She walked up to the buggy and took a beautiful beaded necklace off. The necklace had a small pocket and she put some sage brush in it. She hugged the boys, tears fell in the pocket, and in the Paiute language she told them that this would keep them safe and bring them home. She hung the necklace on the wagon and walked back to the camp. About everyone in the Owens Valley had heard what had happened to the Bakers and they were very happy to see how well Joe Baker and the two boys were doing. They traveled fast with the light buggy and the young team.

Joe Baker was amazed at how the country was growing. There were farms, ranches, fields of grain, and orchards where it had been nothing but sage brush and rocks when he and Katy had come to the valley. The towns were growing and there was even talk of bringing the railroad in. When they got to Dunmovin, they spent two days with the Stewarts. Minnie was delighted to have the company and have the boys. She had heard about Katy and was very happy to see how well Joe was handling things on his own. She asked them to bring her some citrus fruit on their return. She stood by the gate and watched until they went out of sight.

Joe Baker had his gold hidden in the bottom of the grain sack in the back of the buggy. He was a little nervous when he passed Robbers Roost and Vasquez Rocks, but there was no trouble. When they got to the San Fernando Valley, it was the first time the boys had ever seen oranges. limes, and grapefruit. Joe stopped by a farm and bought some oranges. When they arrived at the Baker farm, the whole family was there to greet them. Walter's young cousins had never seen an Indian before and only had heard wild stories about them. It wasn't long, however, before they were running and playing like all children do.

Joe deposited his gold in the bank and bought clothes hats and boots for himself, the boys, and Little Bean and Jimmy. He, also, bought a few dresses for Hummingbird and the women that helped her with the garden. He bought a new skinning knife with seven inch blade for the chief.

Joe and the boys spent a few days with Katy's

parents and a few with Joe's brothers. They talked far into the night after the kids were in bed. Joe told them how the wildlife was multiplying and about the golden trout in the high country. He told them that he was taking the boys to the cow camp when they got home. Grandpa Baker bought the boys new fishing poles.

It was soon time to leave and the horses knew they were heading home. They covered the miles in no time. When they arrived at Dunmovin, they delivered the oranges Minnie wanted and stayed for two days. Minnie spoiled the boys with sweet milk and all the cookies they could eat. When it was time to leave, she held them in her arms and tears rolled down her cheeks as she said goodbye.

As soon as the travelers pulled into the Baker farm, the boys jumped out and headed for the camp with a sack of oranges for Hummingbird. They showed her how to peel and eat them and she shared them with the tribe. They had never seen anything like them and the sack of fruit didn't last long.

The boys were excited about going to the cow camp. Joe Baker told them there would be plenty time to play, but the work came first. They rode into the cow camp in the afternoon and put up a tent. The boys wanted to sleep out in the meadow, but when Little Bean started telling bear stories, they decided to stay in the tent.

In the morning, the crew put a harness on the work horse and pulled in trees to build corrals and logs for fire wood. They cut and stacked wood all afternoon, then they grabbed their fishing poles and headed for the lake. The boys kept the three men busy cleaning, salting and drying the fish. Joe Baker was going to let the boys sell some of the trout when they got back to the valley.

Time was going fast and it was soon time to get back to the farm. The boys wanted to stay with Little Bean and Jimmy the rest of the summer, but Joe Baker knew Hummingbird would be upset. He told them they could come back in the fall to bring the cattle out.

The wheat was ready to harvest when they got home. A few sacks of wheat were kept for chicken feed and the rest was hauled to Round Valley to be ground into flour. Mr. Jones kept six sacks for payment. Most of the flour was sold on the way home and the rest was stored in the cellar. The rest of the fall harvest was done and it was time to bring the cattle out of the high country. The tribe was getting ready to head for their camp in Wacoba.

Once again, the weather held in the high country. The nights were cold, but the days were warm. The aspen trees were turning gold. Fishing and hunting was great. The boys were getting big and helped drag the deer down to where Joe Baker could get a mule to it to load it on. They were learning to skin the deer and to take care of the hides. They were enjoying the weather as they packed up and got ready to leave at the first sign of snow.

Joe Baker was looking forward to the sheep heading south. He wanted to show Mr. Yribarren his mules. The big work mares and four saddle mares all had mule colts.

Over in the Inyo Mountains, the tribe was enjoying a good harvest. The pinion trees were loaded with nuts. They had two rifles in camp and were able to bring down four mountain sheep and six deer. Some of the tribe stayed at the Wacoba camp and gathered nuts and made jerky. Some were going to the Valley of Salt. Hummingbird wanted to go for salt as she would enjoy camping at the hot springs for a few days.

When they arrived at the hot springs, Hummingbird noticed a very poor looking camp with several children and a man from the Shoshone tribe. The Paiutes and Shoshones had traded for centuries and could speak both languages. The man's wife had died and he had been very sick and could not feed his family. Hummingbird and some of the other women each took one of the children to their own camp. The oldest boy would stay with his father. The men of the tribe gave the boy a good bow and plenty of arrows. When the tribe went back to Wacoba, they left the old man and his son enough jerky and pine nuts to last the winter.

Hummingbird had chosen a girl about the same age as Walter and little Joe. She was happy to have a girl as the boys were growing up and spending most of their time working on the farm. She called the girl Haiwee.

A light snow was falling up at the cow camp and they were busy packing up to leave in the morning. The cattle had all been gathered on the big meadow in the morning. Joe Baker and Walter packed the mules Little Bean, Jimmy and Little Joe lined the cattle out and headed for the valley.

When they got to the farm, Joe Baker told the boys to take the food they had for them to the camp. Hummingbird came out to meet them and Haiwee was with her. The boys were, at the point in their lives, when girls were their favorite subject. It was puppy love at first sight. They sure liked her and she seemed to enjoy the attention.

The years were going by and the boys were kept busy on the ranch, branding the calves, breaking the colts, and working in the garden. Every time they were alone, they talked about Haiwee. Little Joe said, "I will marry her. I will be chief someday and we will live at the camp."

"No, she will live with me in the house, I will own the ranch someday."

"No, you are a white man."

So what, lots of white men have Indian wives."

That's the way it went all winter. Hummingbird was teaching Haiwee to cook and make baskets. Haiwee was always busy. She looked after the young children, gathered fire wood, made tea for the elders, and helped them anyway she could. The tribe loved her. She had become a beautiful young woman. It was hard to keep the boys on the job. Every time they got a break, they jumped on their horses and raced to the camp. One day they rode into camp and Haiwee jumped up and put a blanket over something. They asked what it was, but she just smiled and said, "It's a gift."

On the way down the hill, Little Joe said, "I wondered what she's making for me?"

"No, I think it's for me. She sure likes me."

"No, I will be chief someday."

"I will own the ranch someday."

It went that way day after day. After work one day they rode into camp, Haiwee was smiling. She had something behind her back. She had a small basket full of wild roses and a dream catcher necklace. She walked by Little Joe and handed Walter the basket and put the necklace around his neck. That started the argument and soon it came to blows. The chief stepped between them, "Stop, you are brothers give me your arms." They held out there arms and with his knife the chief made a cut on each arm and held the cuts together. "You are blood brothers. Only ishia, the coyote, fights his brother."

Walter got on his horse and rode down to the creek. He was sitting on a rock when Little Joe rode up and they sat side by side. "The chief is right. We will never fight again. Let's go back to work."

Chapter Eleven
WAR

Jess Summers was coming from Bodie to buy cattle. The Baker crew was holding cattle in the corral. Jess rode up with ten men.

"Why the big crew Jess?"

"Have you heard the news Baker?"

"No, what's going on?"

"There's an uprising brewing. Chief Bowers came over from Deep Springs with the warning that he can't control the young men and there's been trouble up north."

"I've not heard a thing, but Little Bean and Jimmy have not been to work for three days."

"That's your warning. They say Joaquin Jim from the other side of the Sierra has the local tribes ready to fight. Baker, I brought extra gold and I will buy everything you have in the corral."

"Is it that bad?"

"Yes, and it'll get worse. They're coming in from every side.

Joe Baker
made a deal on the herd and Jess paid him in gold.

"Jess, don't say anything to the boys. I'll deal with them later."

They helped the Summers crew get the herd started north and wished them luck. The boys wanted to know why he had sold all the cattle. He told them the price of cattle is very high. He said they still had the old cows on the river and they would buy young ones when the time was right.

Joe Baker sat up late that night thinking about what to do. He put his gold, important papers, some clothes, and blankets in pack bags. He put the horses in the corral. In case he decided to go, he would have to travel fast. In the morning he sent the boys to the river to check on the old cows. The Magees rode in and told him they had met Jess Summers and they were having trouble with the Indians at Big Pine Creek. They helped them get through and on their way. "Baker, you have to get the boy out of the valley. Warriors are coming in from all sides. Chief Shondow and Butcher Knife are raiding the mills along the river. Chief Old Hungry is attacking the miners in the Cosos. Take Walter and leave tonight."

"I have to take them both. They've been

together since birth."

"Baker, we know how you feel, but the Indians killed Mrs. McGuire and her little son at Haiwee Meadows. They set the house on fire when they ran out. They shot them full of arrows. There are white men shooting every Indian they see and Little Joe would be safer here. You must go. The warriors are coming in from Nevada and they have guns."

"Where are they getting guns?"

"There are merchants in Aurora doing a thriving business selling guns and ammunition to them. Their names are Wingate and Cohn. I think they are going to hang them."

When the Magees left, Joe Baker thanked them for the information. He was still troubled about leaving Little Joe. He had raised him like a son. The boys rode in and unsaddled. Little Bean walked down from the camp, he did not look at Joe Baker or Walter, he walked up to Little Joe. "The chief wants you in camp. Little Joe looked puzzled, but followed Little Bean up the hill.

This was all Joe Baker needed, he told Walter to go pack up everything he wanted to take. Don't look around and don't hurry. Put your things in the pack bags in the barn. We're leaving."

"What about Joe?"

"We'll talk about it later. Now get moving, but move slow and try not to look suspicious."

When Little Joe walked into the camp, he saw the young braves gathered around a man he had never seen before. The man's face was painted with white streaks on both cheeks and he was waving a tomahawk and talking very loudly to the young braves. Little Joe walked over to his mother and Haiwee who were busy gathering up and getting ready to move their camp. "Mother, what is going on?"

"We're moving further up into the hills to a new camp."

"Who is that man with the war paint and what is he doing here?"

"That's Joaquin Jim. He's from the other side of the great mountains. He said the white men have killed most of his tribe and ran the ones they didn't kill high in the mountains to live like animals. He said the whites will do the same thing to us.

"But, Mother, we have lived in peace with the

white people for years."

"That's what the elders are saying, Son, but they're being shouted down by the young braves. Haiwee and I are moving higher into the mountains."

Hummingbird embraced her son, picked up what few belongings she could carry, and headed up the mountain. Little Joe didn't realize it, but, it was the last time he would ever see his mother and Haiwee.

As soon as it got dark Joe Baker and Walter saddled their horses and packed up, they turned the milk cows, horses, mules and chickens loose. Joe Baker walked over to Katy's grave by the creek and bid farewell to her and the Owens Valley. When they got on their horses they could see a big fire and hear a war dance going on up at the camp. They called the dogs and left.

The war dance lasted all night. Just before daylight. the braves were ready to fight. They picked up their weapons and told Little Joe to get his bow and come with them. They headed for the Baker farm. Little Joe held back and hid in the brush. He went back to the camp but, the women were taking down the camp and were moving it up into the hills. Little Joe saw the flames from the fire down at the ranch, but he didn't hear any gun shots. The dogs were not barking and he hoped the Bakers had left the ranch.

When the warriors returned, they were hostile, they wanted blood. They knew someone had warned the Bakers. When they got to the camp, Little Joe was sitting there and they yelled at him, "You warned them, you coward."

"Joe yelled back at them, "How could I warn them? I didn't know myself until this morning."

"You didn't come with us, you are a coward. You sit in camp, same as squaws."

"Kill him. Don't waste arrows. Use rocks, stone him to death."

They stripped off Little Joe's clothes and tied him to a tree. They gathered rocks to kill him." The chief stepped in, "Stop! What do you say Little Joe?"

"I say I will not fight my brother. I have a scar on my arm, cut by you. You said do not fight my brother."

The chief stood there in silence, then said. "I

did say these words."
The sub chief stepped in, "We listen to our chief. He had only one brother. He should kill the others. He sits in camp like a squaw."

The chief turned to Roadrunner, "Run to the new camp and bring back squaw dresses." They made Joe put on a dress. The chief told him, "You now are Squawbuck Joe. If we ever see you doing men's work or wearing men's clothes, we will kill you." They threw the dresses that Roadrunner had brought. "Take your dresses, Squaw." They threw sticks at him and spit on him.

Joe went down to the farm. Everything was burned and still smoking. He hid by the creek, hoping his brother would come back. He rummaged through the burn at night, he found a knife, two blankets and a canteen. He picked up some rope and made a pack he could carry on his back. He had to find something to eat. When night fell, he went to the river and hid in the tules. He pulled up tule roots and ate them. Joe could hear gun fire everyday and wanted to get away that night. He left the river and went into the Inyos. At the first camp, he found some pine nuts and salt.

He knew where the traps were and set six of them, baited with pine nuts. When he checked the traps he had four squirrels. He skinned them and was so hungry he that ate the hearts and livers raw. The meat was salted and hung up to dry.

The sun came up hot the next day. By afternoon the meat was dry. It was the first meal he had in several days. Three more squirrels and a rabbits were added to his catch the next day. Now he would talk to Winneduma. He took a rabbit foot for an offering to the Great Spirit, as he prayed an Eagle landed on top of Winnedumah. He saw that it was a sign from the spirits.

"Brother Eagle, (Quing-ah) please show me the way to my brother," prayed Little Joe.

The Eagle lifted his wings and rose in the sky, he circled, getting higher and higher until he disappeared in the clouds. A tear streamed down Joe's cheek; he knew he would never see his brother again.

Chapter Twelve
CHARLIE TAYLOR

The fighting was going on up and down the Owens Valley and down into the Cosos. Bend City was burned to the ground. Fighting broke out near Independence. Chief Shandow was killed. Farmers were killed at Big Pine. The Paiutes were calling in help. Soon they had five hundred to a thousand warriors at Bishop Creek where sixty-three settlers faced them and were turned back. Three white men were killed.

Lieutenant Noble came to the valley with fifty men to reestablish Camp Independence. Mr. and Mrs. Summers, Alney Magee and his mother and young niece, and Negro Charlie Taylor were traveling south with a herd of cattle. The women were riding in the wagon when they were attacked by Indians south of Fish Springs. The wagon got stuck in the river and the horses were cut loose and the women were put on the horses. The men ran beside them and made it to Camp Independence.

Charlie Taylor tried unsuccessfully to catch one of the loose horses. He ran to a small butte and fought until his ammunition was gone. Charlie was a veteran of many Indian wars. When he saw the Indians were going to set the butte on fire, he walked out with his hands up and was killed. (Charlie's Butte bears his name today).

Chapter Thirteen
SPIRIT OF THE LION

There was no safe travel in Owens Valley. The mines and mills were closed down. Farms were abandoned. The Calvary was searching the hills and mountains for Indian camps.

White men would kill him. His own people humiliated him and wished him dead. He was entirely alone in the world. He sat looking at the valley until he fell asleep.

Squawbuck Joe wandered back to the north, moving slowly and checking his traps. He dried the meat when he would catch an animal. As he was filling his canteen at the spring a few days later, he saw a lion track. He knew the lion would find a deer. He needed hides to make moccasins and knew that all he had to do was wait. The birds would take him to a kill. He would follow the birds (tracks in the sky). He watched the sky for hours and saw two crows begin circling. Soon two more showed up and the birds landed on a rock not far from the spring. Joe could hear them calling and he made his way to where the crows were. The lion had killed a deer and fed on it. It had covered the carcass with brush and was sleeping nearby. The lion woke up when Joe slowly walked up with a large bush in each hand. He held the bushes high over his head and the eyes of the man and lion met. Joe spoke softly, "Brother Lion, I need your help. I am not allowed to have weapons. I must have meat and hides. May I have what you left?"

The lion held his gaze a few seconds, then climbed a tree and snarled at Joe as he skinned the deer and cut the meat in strips for jerky. He took the brains to tan the hide. He left the bones for the coyotes, scraps for the crows, and a large chunk of meat for the lion. He thanked the lion for the meat and the hide and he thanked the crows for showing him where to find the deer.

Joe needed tools to tan the deer hide. He knew where the tools were hidden at the Wacoba Camp. It took him two days to walk to the site. The Calvary had been there and destroyed the camp. They had broken the grinding stones and burned the pine nuts that were stored there. They had not found the tools, Joe took the scrappers he needed and left the rest. He looked at the camp and remembered all the good times they had there in the fall -- playing hand games, singing, dancing, and feasting. He shook his head and slowly walked away.

The lion had killed another deer when Joe got back to the spring. He needed more salt and he needed moccasins because his feet were bleeding, so he went to the Valley of Salt and the hot springs. He got to the Valley floor, but had to wait until dark to get to the spring as the ground was too hot for his feet. When he got to the springs, he put the hides in to soak and got into the water himself and laid there for hours. Before daylight, Joe went to the salt field and brought back what he needed. There were a few small animals at the spring, so he set some snares.

Flocks of dove were coming in for water at a small pond where the water was cool. Joe made a small teepee beside the pond and put brush over all the water except in front of the teepee. When a flock of dove came in for water, he reached out of the tepee and grabbed them. He caught all the dove he could eat. He picked them and put them in the hot spring for an hour. He pulled them out of the water and put salt on them. It was the first hot meal he had since he left the farm because he had no way to make a fire.

Joe took the deer hides out of the water. The hair had slipped from the hides, so he scraped them and let them dry in the sun. Next, he rubbed them with the deer brains. He was ready to make his moccasins. He cut thin strips to sew with. He cut around his foot for the sole. He cut the tops and laced them together. He made the moccasins extra large so they could be stuffed with rabbit fur in the winter.

Joe would have liked to stay at the hot spring. but he had to gather nuts for winter and hoped the lion would give him more hides. He was ready for winter when the snow came and went back to the hot spring and made a shelter away from the spring. People came to the spring and to get salt, but Joe would hide until they left. He had food to last the winter and was catching doves and a few ducks. At night he bathed in the hot spring.

Chapter Fourteen
SOME CALL HIM SQUAWMAN

The fighting in Owens Valley was winding down. Some of the natives were working on farms and ranches. Indian Agent Wasson was trying to get them to come to the reservation and some were coming in. There were renegades in Round Valley ready to make a last stand. Chief Joe Bowers, who was a scout for the army, was sent in and he told the natives that the army would mow them down like grass. He was able to talk them into laying down their arms and they agreed to a peace settlement.

Indian Agent Wasson and J.H.P. Wentworth, agent for the Southern District of California, held a big powwow at Fort Independence. Wentworth, with Alex Cody as guide and interpreter, brought provisions and presents. They sent runners to the Rancherias and Indian bands calling for a council at Fort Independence. The natives asked only that they be given protection and means of support. They were assured of it. A treaty was made. The natives celebrated with a big fandango.

Squawbuck Joe knew nothing of the treaty. He stayed hidden in the Inyos and Saline Valley. Time meant nothing to Joe and the years went by. He had many camps around the hills and valley. All were stocked with food and tools. He was very careful to brush out his tracks when coming or going from his camps. When the sun went down in the evening he would toss small bits of obsidian to the four winds and pray that someday he would find Walter and Joe Baker and return to the life he loved as a boy. At night, as he lay in his robes, he would wonder if it wouldn't have been better if the tribe had killed him instead of making him live in the hills, hiding like an animal. When the sun came up in the morning, though, he prayed that he could carry his shameful burden and keep the promise he made so long ago.

People were returning to the Owens Valley by the hundreds. The miners were back to work. Farmers were planting fields and orchards and sheep and cattle were being herded through the valley every day. Towns were being built at every major creek. Ben City was never rebuilt. They moved across the river two miles to the west at the site of Putman's and started their town alongside the creek two miles south of Fort Independence. The town was to be called Independence. Tracks were being laid to bring the railroad in from Carson. Sawmills were working overtime to provide lumber. Word had come to Fort Independence that the government would award Chief Joe Bowers six dollars a month pension for his work with the army. A group of miners, going to their claims at Wyman Creek, agreed to take the letter to Antelope Springs. When they found the Chief, they read the letter to him. He told the men that he would go to the Fort.

As Chief Bowers prepared for the trip, he decided to travel down the Inyo Range. It had been a few years since he and his tribe had used the old camps and he wanted to see them again. When he got to the first spring, he saw a very large barefoot print that he could tell was fresh. He tied up his horses. The chief was a tracker and hunter, so he followed the tracks as silently as a lion. He saw a very large man in a woman's dress taking a rabbit out of a trap. He had heard the story, but had never seen the man. He walked slowly up behind him. "You Squawbuck Joe?"

Joe was startled and grabbed his knife. It was the first human voice he had heard for a very long time. The chief held up his hands and he spoke quietly in Paiute. He told Squawbuck Joe that the war was over and there was no more fighting. They camped that night at the spring. The chief had goat meat, bread and cheese. Joe could not remember when he last ate cheese and bread. He asked the chief if he knew where Joe Baker and Walter had gone. The Chief said, "I'll ask at the Fort."

In the morning, Chief Bowers asked, "Will you go with me?"

Squawbuck Joe said, "No, but I will think about it."

"I'll be back. Do you want man's clothes?"

"No, they will kill me."

The chief nodded his head that he understood.

"Bring cheese and bread."

Chief Bowers rode through Badger Flats and down Masourka Canyon. He watered his horse at Barrel Springs and rode to the Fort Independence. He collected his pension and asked about the

Bakers, but no one knew where they were. He bought some cheese and bread at the Edwards Store and headed back to Wacoba.

When the chief arrived back at Squawbuck Joe's camp, he told Joe no one knew where the Bakers were. They ate the food the chief had brought and went to sleep. When the sun came up the chief asked Joe, "Are you coming with me?"

"I'll go. I've been alone too long. If they kill me, okay.

"Nobody will harm you. I am chief. I have good friends in Big Pine."

As they made their way down to the valley, out of the Inyo Range, Joe was amazed and became frightened. The chief had to stop several times to talk Joe out of turning back. The narrow gage railroad had built tracks through the Owens Valley. One can only imagine how frightening it would be to see a huge iron animal coming at you full speed, blowing steam, and sounding like someone being killed, as it rolled into the station.

The chief put his hand on Joe's shoulder and asked him to remember when he and the Bakers drove cattle in the hot sun and the dust. Joe nodded. "Well, now they put the cattle on that big thing and haul them to market far away."

When Joe saw the men loading the cattle and many other things onto the train he told the chief, "Okay, we go."

When the chief and Joe got to the Owens River, they took the packs off of the horses and lead them to water. A big stage coach pulled up and stopped to water the team. The driver was Vernon Smith. When he saw Chief Joe Bowers, he called, "Hey, Chief, long time, no see. Who's that with you?"

"Squawbuck Joe."

"Well, I haven't heard of him for years. I just thought he had died."

"No, Vern, he's been hiding out in the Inyos in the summer and down in Saline
in the winter."

"Where you taking him? Big Pine?"

"I'm going to see if somebody will give the poor guy a chance to have a life."

"Better get that dress off him."

"No, Vern, he made a promise many years ago and he'll never break it."

"Well, Chief, I better get going. They're

starting to bring automobiles in to the valley. I don't know how much longer people will want to ride in a stage coach. Times are changing, Chief. Well, good luck to you and your friend." Vern cracked his whip and headed to the train station, maybe for the last time.

As they rode toward Big Pine Squawbuck Joe was amazed. He remembered, as a young boy, when his brother, Walter, and Little Bean and Jimmy rode to Mono County to bring obsidian to the tribe. There had been nothing but sage brush. Today there were farms, ranches, orchards, and vineyards. The valley was green from one end to the other. There was a large chicken ranch that shipped poultry and eggs on the train to the markets in Los Angeles and they had a large restaurant that served chicken dinners.

It was an odd sight when Chief Joe Bowers rode into Big Pine followed by a huge Indian man wearing a dress, but the chief was well respected and people only looked as they rode by. They rode to the Eugly store and he motioned to Joe to sit on the porch. He went in to talk to Mr. Eugly who had heard of Squawbuck Joe and felt sorry for him.

The store owner told the chief to bring him in. Joe spoke good English and answered everything Mr. Eugly asked and Mr. Eugly told him what his duties would be. He, also, said that he had a shed in the back of the store where he could live if he wanted to work. Chief Joe Bowers went back to Antelope Springs and Squawbuck Joe became a citizen of Big Pine.

Joe kept the store spotless. He helped Mr. Eugly with the heavy lifting. He cooked his meals on the outside stove under the grape arbor. All of the Paiutes knew about Squawbuck Joe, but the men never spoke to him. He was a favorite with the women, though. He carried heavy loads for them and them with their washing and ironing on hot days. In the early days, it was the custom for Indian women to do washing and ironing for families in town and farms and ranches. If one of them was ill or did not show up for work, Joe would fill in. In turn, the women taught him how to weave and he made beautiful baskets that are on display at the Independence Museum today. Joe never spoke unless someone spoke to him. He learned that they had stocked fish in the river and streams that were free for the catching. He talked to packers that came to the store for supplies. He spoke with outfitters who packed tourists into the mountains to fish in the summer and deer hunters in the fall.

Mr. Eugly sold turkeys in the store, a bird that Joe had never seen before. Mr. Eugly bought the turkeys from farmers who herded them on horseback and grazed them in the foot hills and meadows.

Joe made friends with Wing Foo, a small Chinese man that had escaped death when labor riots broke out in Virginia City. Wing hid in a railroad car and made his way to Zurich, the train station in Big Pine. Like Squawbuck Joe, Wing Foo was welcomed to the community. Wing owned the restaurant in the Butler Hotel next door to Euglys.

Cattle were grazed in the high mountains in the summer and in the foot hills in the winters. The cowboys were a happy bunch. Squawbuck Joe would watch them as they rode in, hooping and hollering, in the evening to have a drink at Black's saloon. Joe was definitely an oddity, but he was well liked. Many felt that he'd been dealt a dirty deal by his own people. Joe made his own dresses and helped the Indian women sew theirs. He was a tall and powerful man, with clean cut features and a stoic expression. His teeth were gleaming white and his hair a glossy black. His piercing eyes looked menacing under heavy brows. A life of being scorned had taught him to look for sneers which he expected and dreaded.

Mrs. Eugly was a refined New Englander and, because Mr. Eugly liked it, she wore her hair parted in the middle with a myriad of corkscrew curls caught up in the back of her head, cascading to her waist. To make these curls was tedious until she taught Joe the fine art of hair dressing. She told her friends that she could never have kept it in this manner without Joe's help.

Joe had learned to stay in the background and control his emotions, but there were times when his tribal instincts burst to the surface. One day a photographer aimed a camera at him, Joe rose to his six feet in fury. "You do that, me kill you." The photographer quickly retreated. Joe was sensitive about his dress as it was a constant reminder in the eyes of his world that he had failed to uphold his position as a man.

Joe's only companions among his people were the women. He sat alone and walked alone. After the day's work was done the Paiute women liked to gather for a game of pangingi of chiptui. Their favorite place to play was in the Eugly orchard. Joe would join them there, seated around a blanket with the small stakes in the center. They would play until darkness would drive them home. You could hear them chattering in the Paiute language, with occasional laughter to show glee or disdain.

Whether Joe ever regretted his act which Paiute men considered cowardice, or whether he even spoke to the Euglys about it, is not known. The Euglys respected him and would not pry. In idle times he would sit and look into space and occasional tear would gleam on his cheek, but his thoughts were his own and his reserve respected.

Squawbuck Joe lived to the age of 75 and was buried in the foothills west of Big Pine. Joe's harsh treatment by his tribe was, to some extent, lessened by the kind and compassionate attention provided by the Euglys and the citizens of town of

Big Pine.

The Baker Ranch, 3 miles west of Big Pine, was homesteaded after Joe and Walter Baker left Owens Valley. It was told that Joe and Walter never returned to the Owens Valley and if they ever knew what happened to Little Joe the facts were lost in history.

Made in the USA
Charleston, SC
26 May 2016